CHECKERBOARD BIOGRAPHIES

# MISTER ROGERS

REBECCA FELIX

Checkerboard
Library

An Imprint of Abdo Publishing
abdobooks.com

# ABDOBOOKS.COM

Published by Abdo Publishing, a division of ABDO, PO Box 398166, Minneapolis, Minnesota 55439.
Copyright © 2020 by Abdo Consulting Group, Inc. International copyrights reserved in all countries.
No part of this book may be reproduced in any form without written permission from the publisher.
Checkerboard Library™ is a trademark and logo of Abdo Publishing.

Printed in the United States of America, North Mankato, Minnesota
052019
092019

THIS BOOK CONTAINS
RECYCLED MATERIALS

Design and Production: Mighty Media, Inc.
Editor: Megan Borgert-Spaniol
Cover Photograph: USPS/AP Images
Interior Photographs: AP Images, pp. 5, 11, 13, 15, 17, 21, 25, 27, 28 (top, bottom right), 29 (top left, bottom);
KUHT/Wikimedia Commons, pp. 23, 28 (bottom left); Rudi Riet/Flickr, pp. 19, 29 (top right); Seth Poppel/
Yearbook Library, p. 9; US Census Bureau/Flickr, p. 7

Library of Congress Control Number: 2018966244

**Publisher's Cataloging-in-Publication Data**
Names: Felix, Rebecca, author.
Title: Mister Rogers / by Rebecca Felix
Description: Minneapolis, Minnesota : Abdo Publishing, 2020 | Series: Checkerboard biographies |
    Includes online resources and index.
Identifiers: ISBN 9781532119392 (lib. bdg.) | ISBN 9781532173851 (ebook)
Subjects: LCSH: Rogers, Fred--Juvenile literature. | Mister Rogers' neighborhood (Television program)--
    Juvenile literature. | Television personalities--United States--Biography--Juvenile literature. |
    Children's television programs--United States--Juvenile literature.
Classification: DDC 791.45028092 [B]--dc23

# CONTENTS

AMERICA'S FAVORITE NEIGHBOR....................................4

FAMILY VALUES ....................................................6

MUSIC & TELEVISION ............................................8

PROGRAM PRO ..................................................10

STUDIES & STORYTELLING....................................12

A NATURAL HOST ..............................................14

A NATIONAL HOST..............................................16

MISTER ROGERS' NEIGHBORHOOD............................18

TITLES & HONORS ............................................22

BELOVED LEGEND ............................................26

TIMELINE..........................................................28

GLOSSARY........................................................30

ONLINE RESOURCES ..........................................31

INDEX ..............................................................32

# CHAPTER 1

# AMERICA'S FAVORITE NEIGHBOR

Fred Rogers was the creator and star of *Mister Rogers' Neighborhood.* This children's educational show is one of the longest-running programs in the history of public television.  It aired from 1968 to 2001. Rogers wrote the **scripts** and about 200 songs for the show.  He also starred as the show's host.

Rogers' show was revolutionary.  He worked with **psychologists** and educators to create a program that would support children's emotional intelligence.  Rogers brought wonder and imagination into his program.  He used puppets and songs to talk about all kinds of topics.

Rogers became a trusted expert on children's education.  He also became a celebrity to fans around the world.  His TV program taught children about kindness, compassion, and respect.  Rogers also encouraged the values of self-worth and healthy relationships.  The man who influenced millions of children spent his own childhood developing these values.

Rogers was known for addressing his young audience with respect and patience.

# CHAPTER 2

# FAMILY VALUES

Fred McFeely Rogers was born in Latrobe, Pennsylvania, on March 20, 1928. Fred loved his hometown. His family was very influential in it. Fred's father, James, was a successful businessman. His mother, Nancy, came from a wealthy family.

The Rogers lived a comfortable life with more than enough money. Fred's parents believed serving others was important. They often shared their wealth with members of the Latrobe community. Nancy would sometimes purchase shoes, eyeglasses, and other necessities for children at Fred's school. Serving others became important to Fred as well.

When Fred was 11 years old, his parents adopted a baby girl named Elaine. But for much of Fred's childhood, he didn't have a sibling to keep him company. He also often had to stay indoors due to **asthma**. Imagination was important to Fred, who described his childhood as lonely. He often played on his own with puppets.

Fred would later name his show's delivery man "Mr. McFeely" (*above*) after his grandfather.

Fred's grandfather, Fred McFeely, helped Fred navigate his childhood. Fred's loneliness often made him feel sad or bad about himself. McFeely taught Fred to feel good about himself. These lessons prepared Fred for a future shaping the lives of millions of children.

# CHAPTER 3

# MUSIC & TELEVISION

As Fred grew up, he became more sure of himself. By high school, he had grown into a good student and musician. As a senior, he was elected to the Latrobe High School student council.

After graduating in 1946, Rogers attended New Hampshire's Dartmouth College for one year. He then transferred to Rollins College in Winter Park, Florida. There, he studied music composition. He also met and began dating classmate Joanne Byrd, a concert pianist.

When Rogers was a senior in college, a visit home to Latrobe had a surprising influence on him. At the time, televisions were becoming popular across the nation. And Rogers' parents had purchased one.

The television fascinated Rogers. He recognized it as the medium of the future. But Rogers disliked that TV shows were often loud and violent. So, he decided he wanted to do something positive with television. He would use it to educate viewers and show love.

In addition to being on the student council, Fred was an editor of his high school's yearbook.

# CHAPTER 4

# PROGRAM PRO

In 1951, Rogers graduated from Rollins with a bachelor's degree in music composition. He immediately sought work in television. Rogers found a job at NBC television station in New York City.

At NBC, Rogers worked on the classical music show *The Voice of Firestone* as an assistant producer. He was soon promoted to **floor director**. As floor director, Rogers worked on several other NBC musical programs.

While working in New York, Rogers remained in contact with Joanne, who was still in school in Florida. In 1952, Rogers and Joanne decided on a lifelong commitment. The couple married that June.

Rogers continued his work at NBC into 1953. That November, a TV station in Pittsburg, Pennsylvania, offered him a job. WQED was the nation's first community-sponsored educational TV station. It was not yet being broadcast. WQED wanted Rogers to help produce its first program **schedule**.

Rogers and Joanne moved to Pennsylvania and Rogers got to work. He produced *The Children's Corner*

Joanne Rogers said she and her husband always had a strong friendship at the base of their marriage.

beginning in 1954. The one-hour show was live and aired daily. It featured music, puppets, and more. Rogers was the show's music composer, organ player, and puppeteer.

# CHAPTER 5

# STUDIES & STORYTELLING

Rogers' many roles on *The Children's Corner* kept him busy. At the same time, he took courses at the Pittsburgh **Theological Seminary**. He studied religion.

Rogers had also become interested in childhood development. So, he began learning from child **psychologist** Margaret McFarland. McFarland was known for using storytelling to teach children.

Rogers spent many hours consulting McFarland. He applied what he learned to *The Children's Corner* **scripts** and songs. In 1955, *The Children's Corner* won an award for best locally produced children's program in the nation. The show aired until 1961.

Rogers graduated from the Seminary in 1962 and became a Presbyterian minister in 1963. However, he kept his career focused on children's educational television. In 1963, Canadian television station CBC hired Rogers to create a new show called *Misterogers*. On this show, Rogers would make his **debut** as a show host!

Many of Rogers' future *Mister Rogers' Neighborhood* puppet characters made their debut on *The Children's Corner.* Among them was Lady Elaine Fairchilde (*above*).

# CHAPTER 6

# A NATURAL HOST

Rogers made his on-screen debut in 1963. On *Misterogers,* he spoke to viewers and to the show's puppet characters. Rogers was a natural host. The show became popular in Canada.

Despite *Misterogers'* success, Rogers decided to return to the US. By this time, he and Joanne had two sons, James and John. The couple wanted to raise their children near family. So, they moved back to Pennsylvania.

There, Rogers created a TV program for the Eastern Educational Network. He brought features from *Misterogers* into the new show, called *Misterogers' Neighborhood.* The show included puppet characters that lived in the "Neighborhood of Make-Believe."

*Misterogers' Neighborhood* first aired in the eastern US in October 1966. The show, and Rogers, became immediately popular with young viewers.

## FAN MAIL

When Rogers was at his most famous, he received about 11,000 fan letters a year. He personally responded to each one.

In each episode of *Misterogers' Neighborhood*, a toy trolley entered the Neighborhood of Make-Believe. Rogers provided the voice for many of the puppets that lived there.

# CHAPTER 7

# A NATIONAL HOST

*Misterogers' Neighborhood* was a hit. In April 1967, a Boston TV station arranged an event for viewers to meet Rogers. Event planners expected about 500 people to show up. But on the day of the event, about 5,000 people came! The line to meet Rogers ran down several streets. Rogers had become a celebrity.

Despite its popularity, *Misterogers' Neighborhood* didn't have enough funding to continue production. When viewers learned the show might go off the air, they were upset. Parents and children wrote letters to the press to voice their support for Rogers' show.

In July 1967, National Educational Television (NET) partnered with the Sears-Roebuck Foundation to fund the show. *Misterogers' Neighborhood* would remain on the air. But now, it would appear on screens across the country! The show first aired on NET on February 19, 1968.

Rogers' national program followed the same format as

**Would you be mine?**
**Could you be mine?**
**Won't you be**
**my neighbor?**

Rogers' song-sweater-sneakers routine opened each episode of his show. This routine became one of the most beloved and recognizable parts of the show.

his regional show. He began each **episode** by entering his home and greeting viewers. He sang a song called, "Won't You Be My Neighbor?" as he changed out of his jacket and into a sweater. He also took off his shoes and put on sneakers.

# CHAPTER 8

# MISTER ROGERS' NEIGHBORHOOD

In 1970, the Public Broadcasting Service (PBS) took over as the television network for Rogers' show. The show got a slight name change, becoming *Mister Rogers' Neighborhood*. PBS aired the show under this name for the next 31 years.

*Mister Rogers' Neighborhood* was not the only educational children's show during these years. But Rogers' show was different from other educational programs. He focused on providing children an emotional education.

Rogers did explore **academic** topics with his viewers. But no matter the topic, his focus was teaching children self-worth. He also focused on the importance of emotions and how to express them in a healthy way.

Rogers had a special disposition that helped these lessons get through to his young audience. He spoke in a calm and soothing manner.

> I like you just the way you are.

13

Rogers gave one of his red sweaters to the National Museum of American History in Washington, DC. Rogers' mother knitted the sweaters he wore on television.

He also spoke slowly. This gave viewers time to think about the things he said.

Rogers wrote the **episodes** of *Mister Rogers' Neighborhood*. And each word he wrote was crafted with care. He would spend hours going over **scripts** with child **psychologists**, including McFarland.

Most of Rogers' viewers were preschool age. Rogers knew children this age often **literally** interpret the things they hear. He wanted to make sure nothing he or his characters said could be interpreted the wrong way. Rogers also wanted to cover serious and important topics in a way his audience could understand.

*Mister Rogers' Neighborhood* taught children real-world lessons. But Rogers presented them in a way that also encouraged imagination. He used characters in the Neighborhood of Make-Believe to help teach the topics explored in each episode.

Rogers' puppet characters also supported his focus on **routine**. From his studies in child **psychology**, Rogers knew **routines** provided children with stability. Viewers were brought into the Neighborhood

## CHILDLIKE WONDER

Rogers became known for his ability to guess the types of questions children might ask. For example, Rogers visited an eye doctor during one episode. He asked if the doctor could see thoughts when looking into people's eyes.

Rogers based the neighborhood in *Mister Rogers' Neighborhood* on his hometown of Latrobe, Pennsylvania.

of Make-Believe in every **episode**. And nearly all of the neighborhood's characters appeared on Rogers' show for more than 30 years.

# CHAPTER 9

# TITLES & HONORS

From *Mister Rogers' Neighborhood*'s first year through its final **episode**, Rogers devoted endless hours to his show. But during all these years, he also kept busy with other pursuits.

In 1968, in addition to hosting his show, Rogers also took on work for the White House! Rogers was named chairman of the Forum on Mass Media and Child Development. This role resulted from the White House Conference on Children and Youth. The purpose of this conference was to promote opportunities for young people to achieve.

In 1971, Rogers formed and became chairman of Family Communications, Inc. This nonprofit company produced *Mister Rogers' Neighborhood*. The organization would later produce other media with the goal of supporting children's emotional growth.

Rogers earned many honors for his work supporting children's education. In his lifetime, he received more than 40 honorary degrees from colleges and universities.

# BIO BASICS

**NAME:** Fred McFeely Rogers

**NICKNAME:** Mister Rogers

**BIRTH:** March 20, 1928, Latrobe, Pennsylvania

**DEATH:** February 27, 2003, Pittsburgh, Pennsylvania

**SPOUSE:** Joanne Byrd (1952-2003)

**CHILDREN:** John and James

**FAMOUS FOR:** creating and starring in the children's educational television program *Mister Rogers' Neighborhood*

**ACHIEVEMENTS:** wrote the **script**, music, and lyrics for *Mister Rogers' Neighborhood*; produced the show and starred as its host; became a national expert on children's education and emotional intelligence

He was often consulted as an expert on children's education and mass media.

Rogers was also frequently honored for his influence in television. His list of related awards includes several Daytime Emmy Awards. In 1997, Rogers also earned a Lifetime Achievement Award from the National Academy of Television Arts & Sciences. In 1999, he was admitted into the Television Hall of Fame.

In December 2000, Rogers taped his final **episode** of *Mister Rogers' Neighborhood*. PBS continued to air the show until August 2001.

Rogers continued to earn honors even after his show ended. In 2002, US President George W. Bush awarded Rogers the Presidential Medal of Freedom. This is the highest honor a US **civilian** can earn. Bush recognized Rogers' commitment to children's education.

> When we can talk about our feelings, they become less overwhelming, less upsetting, and less scary.

That December, Rogers received **devastating** news. He was **diagnosed** with stomach **cancer**. Rogers had surgery in January 2003. But this did little to improve his condition. On February 27, Rogers died in his home in Pittsburgh.

President George W. Bush presented Rogers with the Presidential Medal of Freedom on July 9, 2002.

# CHAPTER 10

# BELOVED LEGEND

In May 2003, thousands gathered in Pittsburgh to celebrate Rogers during a memorial service. Musicians, celebrities, family, and friends shared stories of Rogers. They praised his contributions to children's education.

Rogers' influence endured after his death. In 2012, PBS **debuted** *Daniel Tiger's Neighborhood*. This show is based on Rogers' puppet character Daniel Striped Tiger.

In 2018, PBS celebrated the 50th anniversary of *Mister Rogers' Neighborhood* with a feature about the show. A **documentary** about Rogers was also released. And, Hollywood announced a 2019 film honoring Rogers' life.

Rogers helped advance child education in television and media. He created and starred in a successful television program. But his greatest **legacy** is in the hearts of the millions of children who watched him. He taught them kindness and self-worth. Rogers loved everyone just the way they were, and the world loved him back.

> The world needs a sense of worth, and it will achieve it only by its people feeling that they are worthwhile.

Rogers' legacy lives on in reruns of *Mister Rogers' Neighborhood* on local PBS stations and PBSkids.org. Episodes are also available through some streaming services.

# TIMELINE

**1928**

Fred McFeely Rogers is born in Latrobe, Pennsylvania, on March 20.

**1954**

Rogers begins producing *The Children's Corner.*

**1966**

Rogers debuts *Misterogers' Neighborhood* in the eastern US. He becomes a celebrity to local viewers.

**1951**

Rogers graduates from Rollins College with a degree in music composition. He earns a job at NBC television network.

**1963**

Rogers appears on television for the first time as host of the children's TV show *Misterogers.*

**1968**

Rogers' show airs nationally for the first time on February 19.

**2000**

Rogers tapes his final episode of *Mister Rogers' Neighborhood*.

**2018**

PBS celebrates Rogers with a special feature about his show. A documentary about Rogers is also released.

**1970**

Rogers' program is renamed *Mister Rogers' Neighborhood*. The show airs nationally for the next 31 years.

**2003**

Rogers dies from stomach cancer on February 27.

# GLOSSARY

**academic**—relating to school or education.

**asthma**—a condition that causes wheezing and coughing and makes breathing difficult.

**bachelor's degree**—a college degree usually earned after four years of study.

**cancer**—any of a group of often deadly diseases marked by harmful changes in the normal growth of cells. Cancer can spread and destroy healthy tissues and organs.

**civilian**—a person who is not an active member of the military.

**debut**—a first appearance. To debut something is to present or perform it for the first time.

**devastating**—causing great emotional pain.

**diagnose**—to recognize something, such as a disease, by signs, symptoms, or tests.

**documentary**—a film that artistically presents facts, often about an event or a person.

**episode**—one show in a television series.

**floor director**—a person who communicates between the director and crew to make sure programs run smoothly.

**legacy**—something important or meaningful handed down from previous generations or from the past.

**literal**—following the ordinary or usual meaning of the words.

**psychologist** (seye-KAH-luh-jist)—a person who studies psychology, the science of the mind and behavior.

**routine**—a regular order of actions or way of doing something.

**schedule**—a plan, list of events, or timetable.

**script**—the written words and directions used to put on a play, movie, or television show.

**seminary**—a school where students study to be priests, ministers, or rabbis.

**theological**—relating to the study of religion.

# ONLINE RESOURCES

**Booklinks**
NONFICTION NETWORK
FREE! ONLINE NONFICTION RESOURCES

To learn more about Mister Rogers, please visit **abdobooklinks.com** or scan this QR code. These links are routinely monitored and updated to provide the most current information available.

# INDEX

asthma, 6
awards and honors, 12, 22, 24

birth, 6
Byrd, Joanne, 8, 10, 14

Canada, 12, 14
CBC television station, 12
child psychology, 4, 12, 18, 19, 20, 21
*Children's Corner, The*, 10, 11, 12

*Daniel Tiger's Neighborhood*, 26
death, 24, 26

Eastern Educational Network, 14
education, 6, 8, 10, 12

family, 6, 7, 8, 10, 14, 26
Family Communications, Inc., 22
Forum on Mass Media and Child Development, 22

imagination, 4, 6, 20, 21

Latrobe High School, 8

marriage, 10
McFarland, Margaret, 12, 20
McFeely, Fred, 7
*Mister Rogers' Neighborhood*, 4, 18, 19, 20, 21, 22, 24, 26
*Misterogers*, 12, 14
*Misterogers' Neighborhood*, 14, 16, 17

National Educational Television (NET), 16
NBC television station, 10
Neighborhood of Make-Believe, 14, 20, 21

Pennsylvania, 6, 8, 10, 12, 14, 24, 26
Pittsburgh Theological Seminary, 12
popularity, 14, 16
Public Broadcasting Service (PBS), 18, 24, 26
puppets, 4, 6, 11, 14, 20, 21, 26

*Voice of Firestone, The*, 10

White House, The, 22
WQED television station, 10